Signs of the Times

POETRY BY
Bud Osborn

PRINTS BY
Richard Tetrault

Library and Archives Canada Cataloguing in Publication

Osborn, Walton
    Signs of the times / Bud Osborn ; Richard Tetrault, illustrator.
 Poems.
ISBN 1-895636-71-X
    I. Tetrault, Richard, 1951- II. Title.
PS8579.S33S53 2005   C811'.54   C2005-905975-3

Anvil Press gratefully acknowledges the financial assistance of the B.C. Arts Council, the Canada Council
for the Arts, and the Book Publishing Industry Development Program (BPIDP) for their support of our
publishing program. Anvil Press is Represented in Canada by the Literary Press Group and Distributed by
the University of Toronto Press.

Contact:
"Signs of the Times"   Anvil Press
Paneficio Studios   PO Box 3008
800 Keefer Street   Main Post Office
Vancouver, BC V6A 1Y7   Vancouver, BC V6B 3X5
e-mail: rtetrault@telus.net   info@anvilpress.com

Printed in Canada on 30% recycled paper
Design by David Bircham

Special thanks to the following for their support of this project: Dan Tetrault, Anne E. O'Neil, Ellen
Woodsworth, Leslie Ottavi, Nikolas & Lori Thoman, Andrew Phillips, Carrie Herbert, Donald McPherson
& Landon MacKenzie, Jim Harris, Nancy Sweedler, Don Stuart & Ann Webborn, Maurice Spira,
Mary Boulding, Wynn Tetrault, Dave Diewert, W. & M. McKay, Megan Ellis, Libby Davies, Val Kalk &
Sam Kwan, Paul Ching Lee, Sat Bir Khalsa, Jay Hamburger & Atty Gell.

Table of Contents

Preface

Signs of the times are all around us. But whether we choose to see and act is another matter. I have followed and supported the work of Bud Osborn and Richard Tetrault as it concerns the Downtown Eastside, and broader issues, because it compels me to not forget what is evident and pressing. In this second collaboration Osborn and Tetrault collide their mediums, and produce stunning images and words that provoke an emotional, visual, intellectual and political response. I love their work because they are not apart from what they create. There is no distance, no "other", and no appropriation. Their work portrays compassion, love, power and despair, oppression, but above all, a hope of what can be, for all of us, privileged or not. If this is your first encounter with these two remarkable artists, you will be drawn to learn more of the people, places and experiences of which they write. For those already familiar with the poetry and prose of Osborn and visual art of Tetrault, it is a strengthening and determination to continue the struggle for justice and liberation for all people who are oppressed by a soul destroying system.

The greatest barriers we face are cynicism on the part of those who have the resources and power to make change happen, and hopelessness on the part of those who have had everything stripped from them. *"Signs of the Times"* meets these barriers head on and show us a way through, together.

Libby Davies

Vision

Several years since the release of our first book of poetry
and prints, called ***Oppenheimer Park***, ***Signs of the Times***
continues to focus on themes of the Downtown Eastside.

I did the woodcuts and linocuts for the book over the
past year, at the same time as Bud was writing many of
the poems. Although our themes have obvious links, we
made no attempt to literally 'illustrate' each others work,
opting instead for a collage-like quality throughout and
allowing for the confluence of our personal experiences in
the Downtown Eastside community to come through. This
text/image fusion is a rich vein that we feel we have just
begun to tap.

Retaining several characteristics of the first book, such as
strong textural and design elements, was important to us.
In both publications David Bircham did the fine graphic
layout and design. As well, it is a tremendous honour to
have Libby Davies write the preface. I would like to thank
David, Libby, Esther Rausenberg and Anvil Press.

Richard Tetrault, June 2005

Dedication

I dedicate these poems to the memory of Bruce Eriksen,
Gil Puder, and Sharon Martin.

These personal friends, and courageous activists, on behalf of the
politically and socially marginalized and powerless, sacrificed
much to save lives others target for destruction.

Perhaps the most inspiring political advice I've ever been given
was spoken to me by Bruce, who literally rose from his deathbed
to say, "Fuck 'em!", to those who abandon the poorest and most
afflicted of our citizens to extreme suffering and miserable deaths.

My life was wonderfully transformed because of these human
beings – I miss them very much.

Bud Osborn, June 2005

Signs of the Times

across North America
hand held pieces of cardboard
crudely lettered
or painstakingly printed
express
the lived poetry of poverty

no home
no job
no money
no food
and name
preventable diseases
untreated
because of inability
to pay for relief or healing

signs

reaching from the Atlantic
to the Pacific

please help
God bless you
have a good day
God bless
please help

signs

call to us
beg
plead
pray

for a meagre
but heroic
response

give to all who ask

but they want my money for alcohol
they want my money for drugs

give to all who ask

but there's too many
of these
signs that disclose
and subvert
by their very understatement
the social extermination
of human beings

their sheer physical presence
their faces
their eyes
their likeness
pierce our entertainments
pierce our wastefulness
our priorities
          our conscience

a blind man
homeless
holds a sign
and sees through us
so deeply and clearly
we can't stand it

and demand
public space be made private
and these living signs
driven elsewhere
anywhere
nowhere
by more bylaws
by more police

these living signs
anger
they terrify
because they reflect
our own possibilities
in this anti-human economic system

no food
no job
no money
no home

so we need more
zones of exclusion
more censorship of human beings
who hold
these signs of the times
because
they hold them
for us
all

Oscar

Oscar's dead
Oscar from El Salvador
sitting there
with a cane
and black eye
on Powell Street
said he wanted to talk to me
after the meeting
and though he'd been drinking
sat quietly

until suddenly
Oscar burst forth
with a passionate call to action
a call for us to protest
for jobs
and housing
and decriminalization
and to protest against
the violence of the police
the police
the police

and the old white men
aboriginal
latino
ricer
women
excon
afrocanadian
limping bleeding swollen outcast junkies
one hundred altogether
cheered Oscar

and when he and I sat down
Oscar said he just wanted to make sure
the next protest included
the Spanish speaking people
of Oppenheimer Park

I told Oscar
it was an honour
for me to know him
a hero
a former combatant
of the Farabundo Marti National Liberation Front
who fought the Salvadoran generals
the land owners
the right wing Christians
the CIA
and the U.S. corporations
to a standstill

a smile flashed across Oscar's face
he pulled up his shirt
to reveal a long thick scar
zippered with stitch marks
Oscar said that was where
the soldiers shot him
then tears filled his eyes
and spilled down his face
Oscar said the soldiers
killed his wife

Oscar of the inspired speeches
Oscar who lived in the mud in the rain
Oscar the revolutionary and rice wine drinker
Oscar who died in the war zone of the Downtown Eastside

Oscar *(Recordando a Oscar Rosales)*

Oscar está muerto
Oscar de El Salvador
Sentado alli
Con su bastón
Y un ojo negro
En la calle Powell
Dijo que queria hablar conmigo
Despuès de la reunión
Aun que el habia estado tomando
Estaba sentado y calladito

Hasta que de repente
Oscar se levanto
Con un apasionante llamado a la accion
Unllamado a nosotros
A que protestemos por trabajos y
vivienda
Y a la descriminalizacion
Y que protestaramos contra
La violencia de la policia
La policia
La policia

Y el viejo hombre blanco
Aboriginal
Latino
Arrozero
Mujer
Exconvicto
Afro canadiense
Renqueando sangrando inchado
Inservibles tecatos
Cién todos juntos echaban porras
Ycuando el y yo nos sentamos
Oscar dijo que el solo quería asegurarse
Que en la próxima protesta incluyeran
A personas de abla hispana
Del parque oppenheimer

Yo le dije: Oscar para mi ha sido unhonor
conocerte
Un heroe un ex combatiente
De el Frente Farabundo Marti para la
Liberacion Nacional
quien peleo contra Generales salvadoreños
Contra los terra tenientes
contra los cristianos del ala derecha
contra la CIA
Y contra las corporaciones de estados unidos
Y provoco un paro General

En la cara de Oscar se dibujo una Gran
sonrisa
Se levanto la camisa
Para rebelarme una largo y ancha cicatriz
Como un ziper de marcas de las puntadas
Oscar dijo que ero de cuando los soldados
Lo habian valeado
Luego sus ojos se llenaron de lagrimas
Que se derramaron por su cara
Oscar dijo que los soldados habían matado
A su esposa

Oscar de sus platicas inspiradas
Oscar quien vivio en el lodo, en la lluvia
Oscar el revolucionario y bevedor
De vino de arroz para cocinar
Oscar quien murio en la zona de guerra de
El Downtown Eastside

POEMA ORIGINAL DE BUD OSBORN

TRADUCIDO DEL INGLES A ESPAÑAL POR

MONSERRAT MUÑOZ (MONTY)

Theology from the Outer Darkness

at a street church in the Downtown Eastside
          a middle-aged First Nations man remains
after the service and hot dogs
          and says he wants to speak to someone
he then tells me
          his family is dying
of AIDS from dirty needles
          and overdose deaths

"my family is dying right now" he says
          "in the bar
on the street"
          and the man's face
streaked with scars
          creases in anguish
he sticks his arms straight out at his sides
          and makes sounds
of spikes driven through flesh and bone
          ghastly violent sounds
he says "I don't want to give up
          but my brother just died
and he really tried
          to find new life"

and the man nods toward the front of the room
          to the bloody tortured executed Christ
"I think a lot about that gentleman" he says
          and stretches his arms out again

and makes the sounds
          of crucifixion
and says
          "the pain
                    the pain"

14

because
this groundbreaking
breaks
homelessness
into a home
for those
of us
hardest hit
by social heartlessness –

this groundbreaking
breaks
open
a place
in the displacement-driven
social space
for all of us

we need
many more New Portland hotels
for those
among us
who suffer most
and most need a home

but we dearly need
many more New Portland hotels
for those
of us
whose homes can never be truly lived
in
until there is no one
who is homeless

20 West Hastings

so today
we are grateful
because
this groundbreaking
breaks
open
hope for a homecoming
for all
of us

THE PORTLAND HOTEL SOCIETY
IS UNIQUE AS FAR AS I KNOW IN
HOUSING AND CARING FOR PEOPLE
WHO WOULD NOT HAVE ANYWHERE
ELSE BUT THE STREETS TO LIVE. THE
HOTEL / RESIDENCY HAS NO RULES
FOR OCCUPANCY, OTHERWISE FEW OF
THE RESIDENTS COULD LIVE THERE.
INSTEAD, PEOPLE ARE RESPONSIBLE
FOR THEIR ACTIONS, BUT NOTHING
THEY DO COULD CAUSE THEM TO
LOSE THEIR ROOMS. COMPASSION
IS EMBEDDED IN THE DELIVERY OF
SERVICES. I WAS HONOURED TO BE
ASKED TO WRITE AND SPEAK THIS
POEM FOR THE GROUND-BREAKING
CEREMONY OF A NEW AND EXPANDED
BUILDING REPLACING THE OLD AND
DECREPIT HOTEL THAT WAS
FORMERLY USED
— BUD

she who was a child
beloved of life
has now become a slave
she screams at night
she raves during the day
and among all her men
there is none to comfort her
all her friends have betrayed her
they have become like enemies
and after this affliction
and harsh servitude in the Downtown Eastside
she is going into exile
she is being driven out
and will find no resting place
all those who greedily pursue her
have overtaken her
in the midst of her suffering
and no one comes to celebrate life with her
all her streets are cruel
her representatives fight among themselves
her advocates grieve
and she is in bitter anguish
her real enemies have become her masters
her real enemies are taking it easy
her children have been stolen from her
her beauty has been corrupted
her dreams of life are like eagles

that find no nests
in weariness they have flown away
but in these days of her affliction and drunkenness
she remembers the hours of joy and moments of peace
that were hers in the past
before she and her people
fell into enemy hands
and there was no one to help her
her enemies now look at her
and laugh at her destruction
she herself commits crimes
she herself makes choices that bring death
instead of more life
but she has been brutalized
she has been stripped naked
and thrown into the streets

where she is mocked and dishonoured
as one diseased and unwanted
she herself groans
and turns her face from the mirror
she did not take this day seriously enough
her destruction is astounding
her destruction is an abomination
and there is no one to comfort her
"look at me! see my face!" she pleads for help
but the enemy has triumphed

Downtown Eastside

the enemy is laying hands
on her heart and her soul and her flesh
she sees predators of all kinds
enter her streets
all her people groan
as they search for bread
they barter their lives for what they need
to relieve their suffering
to keep themselves alive
she says "look at me and please consider me
for I am despised and forsaken and abandoned"

she who was a child
beloved of life
has now become a prostitute for her enemies
and she says
"am I nothing to you, you who pass by?
is my suffering any less deserving of relief
than others?"
this suffering that a cold inhuman system
has inflicted upon me
allows epidemics of death
in my blood
it has made me think of suicide
day and night
it has kept hope far from me
and this is why I act desperately

this is why my eyes burn with fear
and my eyes are dark and disturbing
with anger
and my eyes are crushed
with despair
and my eyes pour down painful tears
for there is no one near to comfort me
no one is here to restore my life
and my children are becoming destitute with me
because the enemy has prevailed
and the Downtown Eastside stretches out her hands
but there is no one to comfort her
the Downtown Eastside has become
an object of loathing and derision
to her neighbours
and to those who could rescue her
and what is worse
to herself

the visions of politicians
are self-seeking and destructive
to us
their words are worthless
their meetings are humiliating
the advice they give
and the questions they ask
their seeming concern

are deceitful and hypocritical
and they laugh at us
they pass through the Downtown Eastside
and shake their heads
but
were we not once children
born beloved of life
and now become no better than
objects to be kicked and manipulated?
social failures to be whipped by this cruel system?
and our good friends
our enemies
they say 'we are swallowing up the Downtown Eastside
we will drive the low-life out
this is the day we wait for
to make our city a city for tourists and corporations
this is the day we work for
when we drive out the bad poor
and drive out their agencies
except for the good poor
who will live quietly and intimidated
in enclaves of social housing'
and our enemies gloat over how easy it is
to destroy our community
how easy it is
to divide our community
how easy it is

the hearts of the people of the Downtown Eastside
cry out
oh hard-pressed homes of the
economically poor and politically powerless
let your tears fall like November rains
day and night
give yourself no distraction or sedation
give your eyes no rest
arise! come alive! resist!
cry out in the night
as the pressure on our lives increases
pour out your heart like hail
so that all will hear and feel and see
let us lift up our lives
for the lives of all of us
who walk hungry and oppressed
at every street corner
look oh city of Vancouver
look oh politicians and planners and bankers
and developers
whom have you ever treated like this?
would you tear your children away
from their mothers' breasts
would you deny life to them
as you do to the Downtown Eastside?

people all over have heard my suffering cries
but there is no one to comfort me
no one to comfort the community of the poor
in the Downtown Eastside
all my enemies have heard my pleas and anguish
but they are satisfied
at what they are bringing about
so may they experience
what is happening to me
may their lies and greed and politics and manipulations
and their hardness of heart
and their abandonment of the Downtown Eastside
come back to haunt them
come back to tear their 'communities' apart
come back to drive them to acts of desperation
come back to make them objects of scorn
come back upon them to destory their lives
with no one to comfort them
no one to help them
for my pain is immense
and my heart is racing
and my heart is weary

THIS POEM WAS WRITTEN IN 1997 WHEN THE SITUATION IN THE DOWNTOWN EASTSIDE WAS LITERALLY AS HORRIFIC AS DESCRIBED. AS A DIRECTOR ON THE VANCOUVER / RICHMOND HEALTH BOARD, I WAS AS ABLE, IN 1997, AGAINST BUREAUCRATIC OPPOSITION, TO HAVE A MOTION PASSED DECLARING VANCOUVER'S FIRST-EVER PUBLIC HEALTH EMERGENCY, BECAUSE OF THE PANDEMICS AND OVERDOSE DEATHS BESIEGING THE DOWNTOWN EASTSIDE. SINCE THEN, RESIDENTS OF THE DOWNTOWN EASTSIDE AND PEOPLE IN VANCOUVER AND ELSEWHERE HAVE INDEED RESPONDED TO INHUMAN SUFFERING WITH CONCRETE INITIATIVES INTENDED TO RELIEVE IT. THOUGH MANY BATTLES ARE YET TO BE FOUGHT, THE PRESERVATION AND STRENGTHENING OF A RARE AND IMMENSELY IMPORTANT COMMUNITY OF ECONOMICALLY IMPOVERISHED, BRUTALLY AFFLICTED AND EXTRAORDINARILY CREATIVE AND COMMITTED HUMAN BEINGS, IS MUCH CLOSER TO ENDURING THAN IT APPEARED 8 YEARS AGO. WHILE THE POEM SPECIFICALLY NAMES THE DOWNTOWN EASTSIDE, THE CIRCUMSTANCES EXPRESSED PREVAIL THROUGHOUT THE WORLD, AND WILL INTENSIFY UNLESS THE NEO-LIBERAL SOCIO-ECONOMIC IDEOLOGY AND ITS INSTITUTIONS, SO RUINOUS OF ALL THAT IS HUMAN AND NATURAL, IS TURNED UPSIDE-DOWN TO FULLY RESPOND TO THE NEEDLESS SUFFERING AND DESTRUCTION OF AUTHENTIC COMMUNITY THIS SYSTEM PRODUCES.
— BUD

a binner approaching a bin
anticipates
something valuable
will be found
among the discarded
rejected
trash and useless
objects
of our society

a binner is not afraid
to be seen
in deep
and intimate relationship
with what others
avoid
like the plague

a binner sees possibility
where others
see the need
for a clean-up campaign

a binner
is a true spiritual guide
so let their example
impel
the rest of us
to go
and do likewise

A Binner is a True Spiritual Guide

TO CARL

23

Jolene
who sat
slumped
in silence
slightly rocking
and weeping
everyday in group therapy

smashed jagged glass
out of her bathroom mirror
and slashed herself
because she was told
she wasn't getting any better
and had to go home

to her
white suburban middle-class
family

but after
her violent rebellion
she looked radiant
and defiant
and was friendly
and outgoing
because she was told that
now
she couldn't
go
back
home

from the Suicide Ward

after a memorial service
for Irving Stein
at Mission Possible
I walk to the restroom
in Oppenheimer Park
and wait outside
for the stalls to empty

a young native woman
a girl really
so radiant and lovely
comes over and says
"I saw you on television last week!"

"oh yeah?" I say

"yeah!" she exclaims
and holds her left arm out
and points to the needle tracks
abscess wounds
and says
"you make us human beings!"

and tells me
she's going into a recovery house
tomorrow
but has already been
in lots of those places

"me too" I say
and tell her
"we gotta keep trying"

she agrees
and says she's afraid
to work the streets now
with so many women
disappearing or being hurt

I apologize to her for getting distracted
but I'm watching ambulance guys
try to revive a white man
who is down on the grass
not moving at all
but suddenly jerks his arms around
and looks very angry
at having his life saved
I know that kind of resentment too

the girl turns around
looks at the scene
laughs
and says
"that's like me
when I overdosed
and woke up
in the ambulance
with a tube
down my throat
and I said
'gimme the money first!'"

we both laugh
at the horror of it all
and tell our names
and put out our hands
and I wish her
good luck tomorrow
and she smiles
like bright new life shining
out of deathliness

I use the can
then walk slowly through the park
past the picnic table
where I last saw Irving
and we waved greetings to each other
just a couple of days
before he was killed
by an automobile

and I look
at the new totem pole
raised to remember
those of us
who've died by violence
in the Downtown Eastside

and I see
waves of crows seagulls starlings and sparrows
fly on and off the grass
flashing into the air
with silver black brown and white wings
like the spirits
of those who've died
stirring the air
for those of us
resisting
our community's
unseen and powerful predators
who produce
so many
forms of death

what do you do
when 'the most hated human being in
society'
is the only man you knew
who loved you
and was your gangster-hero-stepfather
but molested your sister
and was convicted of raping a 9-year-old
girl?

Excruciations of Compassion

or what do you do
when a woman accused of
'flaunting contempt for the moral laws
on which our society ultimately rests'
accused in a full-page sensational
suicide and sex scandal
what do you do
when this most evil woman
is your mother?

or what do you do
when the killer who shot your grandmother in
the heart
is her daughter and your aunt
who turned the gun on herself?

well
it's a hell of a lot easier on me
to condemn some monster/alien/stranger
and revel in self-righteousness
than to have
these excruciations of compassion
and suffer with
the most hated humans
the most immoral women
the most extreme violence
in a scary and confusing
solidarity with the socially damned
that burns so furiously
in my blood

* I WROTE THIS POEM NOT
LONG BEFORE I ATTENDED A
PRISON ABOLITION CONFERENCE
IN TORONTO, ONTARIO.
INTERNATIONAL IN SCOPE (ANGELA
DAVIS WAS ONE WHO SPOKE),
I BROUGHT WITH ME NOT ONLY
THIS POEM, BUT POETRY WRITTEN
BY WOMEN INCARCERATED IN
B.C.C.W. (BRITISH COLUMBIA
CORRECTIONAL CENTRE FOR WOMEN)
IN BURNABY. THE WOMEN HAD
A DAILY AND WELL-ATTENDED
WRITING WORKSHOP, TO WHICH I
WAS INVITED TO PARTICIPATE MANY
TIMES. I BOTH READ ALOUD AND
DISTRIBUTED THEIR POEMS (WHICH
WERE WELL RECEIVED) DURING THE
CONFERENCE. ON MY RETURN TO
B.C. I REPORTED ON THEIR POEMS'
RECEPTION TO THE WOMEN WHOSE
WRITING WORKSHOP WOULD SOON BE
ABOLISHED AMIDST INSTITUTIONAL
RE-STRUCTURING.

THE ORGANIZER OF THE TORONTO
CONFERENCE SPOKE TO ME ABOUT
MY OWN POEM "EXCRUCIATIONS OF
COMPASSION" AFTER I FINISHED MY
PUBLIC READING. SHE THANKED ME
FOR SPEAKING OF THESE PAINFUL
AND COMPLEX SITUATIONS BECAUSE
SHE HAD HERSELF EXPERIENCED
AN ESPECIALLY HURTFUL EVENT
WHEN A YOUNG CONVICT SHE'D
BEFRIENDED WAS RELEASED FROM
PRISON INTO HER CARE; AND
THEN PROCEEDED TO COMMIT A
VICIOUS CRIME, WHICH NOT ONLY
RE-IMPRISONED HIM, BUT SHE WAS
PUBLICLY VILIFIED IN THE MEDIA.
—BUD

The Truth of Community

all day long
the horrible August sun
set them on fire
and machine guns
and attack dogs
and barbed-wire fences wired with electricity
where teenaged boys threw themselves
to escape
from Auschwitz

a prisoner fled the camp
or so the Nazis said
and lined the 600 men of barrack 14 into rows

the men were forbidden to speak
sit down
or take one step out of line
under penalty of immediate execution

all day long

until assistant camp commandant Fritsch arrived
and announced that since
the escaped prisoner had not been found
10 of the men standing there would die

and Fritsch began to walk the rows
examining the prisoners
selecting which of them would be
stripped naked
locked in a cellar half-buried in the earth
and kept there
until they starved to death

one of the condemned men
a young polish soldier
Francis Gajownicek
fell to his knees and cried out
that he had a young wife
and small children
and wanted to live

Fritsch ordered the man to the starvation cell

but then
something extraordinary occurred
something unheard of in Auschwitz

a man stepped forward out of the rows
and began to speak

Fritsch commanded the man to get back into line
"have you gone mad?" Fritsch shouted at him

but the prisoner calmly replied
that he wished to take
Francis Gajownicek's place

the man explained that since he himself
was old and ill
the Nazis could get more work
from a younger man

and assistant camp commandant Fritsch
according to witnesses
fell silent
and appeared stunned

AN AFRICAN-AMERICAN WOMAN IN
TUSCON, ARIZONA TOLD ME THIS
POEM SAVED HER MOTHER'S LIFE.
HER MOTHER HAD DIABETES SO
DISABLING HER LIFE DRAMATICALLY
DETERIORATED AND DOCTORS
SAID THERE WAS NO MORE THEY
COULD DO. BUT WHEN THE
WOMAN'S DAUGHTER READ THE
LINES DESCRIBING THE EFFECTS
OF DEHYDRATION, ESPECIALLY
DISORDERED CONSCIOUSNESS, SHE
SAID AN ILLUMINATION INFORMED
HER OF EXACTLY WHAT TO DO FOR
HER MOTHER. AND THE PROTEIN
SHAKES AND OTHER MINISTRATIONS
SHE PROVIDED ON A DAILY BASIS
RESTORED HER MOTHER'S LIFE
COMPLETELY. THE WOMAN HAS BEEN
REPEATING THIS EXPERIENCE TO
OTHERS — AN EXAMPLE TO ME OF THE
POWER OF POETRY AND THE SPIRIT
OF KOLBE TO INSPIRE HEALING AND
SAVE LIVES.
— BUD

34

the August sun burned the air
and Auschwitz fell silent

Fritsch pondered
then
astonishingly
rescinded his own order
and granted the prisoner's request

and so Maximillian Kolbe joined the other 9 men
stripped of their clothes
and interred in their tomb

Kolbe's own hard-won community of Franciscans
who had housed refugees
fed the poor
repaired the machinery of peasant farmers
and dispensed medicine to any who were in need
had been destroyed
his brothers murdered or sent into exile
and Kolbe incarcerated in Auschwitz

first the brain dehydrates
and hallucinates
but Kolbe remained lucid
and comforted the others
they sang canticles of love
in a death cell
in Auschwitz

and on the 14th day
when Nazis entered the cell
to remove the bodies
Maximillian Kolbe
still alive
had to be killed
with an injection of phenic acid

Kolbe
who created community even in Auschwitz

who lived community while naked and starving to death

who sang community into a situation without hope

who demonstrated that community cannot be destroyed
though buildings are demolished
though people are scattered and lives shattered

who taught that community cannot be extinguished
as long as a single human being
steps forward
out of line
and speaks out
for the sake of another's life

Kolbe

How Cruel are We?

a white girl
is below my balcony
                keeping 6 in the alley
while a Latino man
                shoots up behind her
valuable skin
                so often torn by
objects more comforting
                than our harsh hand
locking her up again and again
                because we cannot stand
to see her love where we do not
                and consequently refuse
to help her

                no help for her
standing in a Chinatown doorway
                leaning defiantly
smoking a cigarette
                and ready
                to not take
                any shit
                        from police
                                whose handcuffs
                                        scar the wrists of   our

abandoned

daughter

No matter how Vicious the System is

the War on Terror
War on Drugs
War on the Poor
are afflictions
and affliction means
causing pain and suffering
and I am a human being
like so many
who have known affliction
in my family
in my nerves
in my thoughts
in my heart
and in the community of the poor
indeed this global economy turns its hand against me
again and again
all day long
and it has besieged and surrounded me
with bitterness and hardship
with isolation and self-destruction and self-centredness
this global economy has made me live in powerlessness
like those long dead
it has walled me in so that I cannot escape it
it has weighed my heart down with chains

and with thoughts it has inflicted into me
so that I become this system of oppression
I make scapegoats of others
I hate and I resent and I fear and I am greedy
and even when I have called out or cried for help
my voice and my wounds are managed by the system
this system of development and theft
has blocked my life with meetings and techniques
of exclusion and control
it has made all my paths hopeless
and like a rapist hiding in the shadows

like a serial killer offering a hand and a smile
this system drags me from the path of real life
and mangles me
and leaves me without help
for my heart
for my life
for my soul
this system of tourism and globalization
this system of war
against 'terror' and the poor
bearing down where I live

makes me a target
for business
for governments and shadow governments
for news media
for free trade and economic warfare
the system has pierced my heart
with lies
and my voice and my anguish and my loneliness
become as nothing
I become a laughingstock to this system
it mocks me in entertainment all day long
it mocks me in newspapers magazines television movies
and advertising
it has filled me with self-contempt
and stuffed me with resentment
it has broken my teeth with indifference
and crushed me into fantasies
and I have no idea what true relationship is
the system reduces me
reduces my imagination my hopes my dreams
reduces me to the size of a disappearing welfare cheque
reduces me to a consumer of death
but I remember my affliction
I remember with bitterness and fear
I well remember
and my soul is knifed within me

yet I also bring something else to mind
and therefore I have hope
because of our deep and hidden and oppressed
love for one another
deeper than any economics of greed and madness
no we are not completely dehumanized
or entirely turned against each other
for true compassion never fails
compassion is new every morning
compassion means suffering with
the one who is different than us
the one who is most like us
and from compassion comes hope
and life is good if we seek to be compassionate
if we seek to understand the other person
and life is good if we live to help each other
without conditions
and life is good
no matter how vicious the system is
if we use our own suffering
to understand others who are in pain
and life is good if we live to defend others
who are weaker and more powerless and more afflicted
than ourselves
and compassion suffers together
not in isolation
as this system would make us behave
and life is good if we become for others

the brother or sister
we may never have had
and life is good if we realize
that our lives are not all right
if the lives of others whom we fear
are distressed or degraded
and life is good if we can see
beyond the reach of the system
that our lives depend
on the lives of others
so perhaps it is not the worst thing
that this system strips us of everything
except what we have in our hearts
for we are not to be without
what our hearts most deeply desire
love
and care
and though we now live grief-stricken and terrorized
so powerful is compassion
that it will overcome this global system
this system denying us our full lives
we will overcome because we live differently
than the system intends for us
we live in cooperation and compassion
and we have arisen
and we have come alive
and we are resisting

A New Day

we of the Downtown Eastside
have made history today
we who have had the highest rate
of overdose deaths
in the world
we today are making history
we who have had the highest AIDS rate in the
world
among injecting junkies
the highest rate of tuberculosis
from shooting up in putrid alleys
and poisonous hotel rooms
are making history
we have won a major battle
we the most afflicted of the poor
have won a battle
in the war against the drug warriors
we have beaten them
in a harm reduction battle
a war of 50 years
begun by Ernie Winch
MLA for Burnaby
who first tried to bring
supervised injection sites to Vancouver

50 years
tens of thousands of needless
deaths and infections
tens of thousands of destroyed families
and hopelessness

but here something new has emerged
from the work sweat blood deaths and
demonstrations
for so many years
from so many people

we are writing a new Canadian history
Canada's real identity
is not tearing apart communities and families
like the United States
that pushes dope
and the death of hope
to enter our land
yes, we have fought for
over 50 years
and today we can announce
an incredible victory
saving lives
and giving those lives
opportunity for change
for a real life
of love and joy
and care and health
and this is what a safe injection site is about
and this is our day
the day for everyone who has ever cared
for the Downtown Eastside
in a world of death and terror
because we have won a corner of it
for life and peace

there has never before been
in North America
an injection site
supported by 3 levels of government
and the local police
until now
this is the beginning of new life
a new illuminating light
for everyone
in the horrific darkness of the
war on drugs in North America
a new illuminating light
of hope

IT WAS A PREVIOUSLY UNHEARD
OF REQUEST AND PRIVILEGE FOR
A POET TO BE ASKED TO WRITE
AND READ A POEM FOR THE
OPENING OF INSITE,
NORTH AMERICA'S FIRST
PUBLICLY-SUPPORTED
SUPERVISED INJECTION SITE.
I THEREFORE DEDICATE THIS
POEM TO THE MANY PEOPLE
WHO LAID DOWN THEIR LIVES TO
BRING ABOUT THIS LIFE-SAVING
AND HOPE-INSPIRING INITIATIVE.
— BUD

"I thought I was just havin a party
but the police told me
I was runnin a crack house!"

Mike's haiku

Richard Tetrault

Photo: Esther Rausenberg

Richard Tetrault has lived and worked in the Downtown Eastside of Vancouver for more than thirty years, making this area of the city a focus for his paintings and prints, as well as the location for many of his public murals.

Tetrault studied drawing, printmaking and painting in Vancouver and New York, and his work has been exhibited and collected both locally and internationally. Recent exhibitions include a print show in Poland (2002), a group travelling print exchange between Europe, Japan and Canada (2005-06) and a twenty-five year retrospective of his work (***Painted Stories: Visualizing the Downtown Eastside***, Interurban Gallery 2003).

Tetrault's murals and public works can be seen on streets, in community centres, public schools and other locations throughout the region. In 1998, He was a coordinator for ***Walls of Change,*** a large, community-based mural project that was designed to give the Downtown Eastside community an opportunity to express its uniqueness and concerns. More recently, he worked with a team of artists on ***Community Walls/ Community Voices*** (2002-2003), a three-block long mosaic and concrete mural on Vancouver's Commercial Drive. In 2005, he participated in a world symposium on mural painting in Tlaxcala, Mexico.

A richly illustrated book showcasing his paintings, prints and murals, called ***Painted Lives and Shifting Landscapes,*** was published in 2005 by Anvil Press.

Bud Osborn has been a poet and social activist for nearly forty years. A former director of the Vancouver/Richmond Health Board, Bud Osborn was instrumental in founding such harm reduction organizations as VANDU (Vancouver Area Network of Drug Users), GTA (Grief to Action), and PRG (Political Response Group), and has been called by Vancouver Mayor Larry Campbell *"the one who started it all"* in the battle for Safe Injections Sites. Recently he has launched Creative Resistance, a group that advocates the repeal of drug prohibition and its "War on Drugs" strategy.

Bud Osborn's poetry credo is "fidelity to lived experience." He has published five books of poetry which include *Lonesome Monsters* (Anvil Press, 1995), *Hundred Block Rock* (Arsenal Pulp, 1999), *Oppenheimer Park* (1998, in collaboration with artist Richard Tetrault), and *Keys to Kingdoms* (Get to the Point, 1999) which won the City of Vancouver Book Award. The title narrative from *"Keys to Kingdoms"* was made into a film-poem that won an award at the Vancouver Film Festival and has been screened internationally at more than 30 film festivals. He has also recorded his poetry and performed with musicians at venues such as the Vancouver Folk and Jazz Festivals, and in Taegu, South Korea.

Photo: Al McKay